10 Things I Learned Shooting Short Films

A Reality Check for First-Time Filmmakers

Kenn Crawford

CRAWFORD HOUSE PUBLISHING
1344 Grand Lake Road, Nova Scotia, Canada B1M 1A1

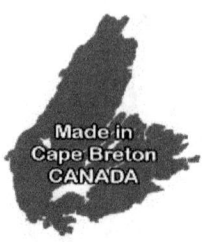

Copyright © 2021 Kenn Crawford

ALL RIGHTS RESERVED. NO PART OF THIS PUBLICATION MAY BE REPRODUCED, DISTRIBUTED, OR TRANSMITTED IN ANY FORM OR BY ANY MEANS, INCLUDING PHOTOCOPYING, SCANNING, RECORDING, OR ANY OTHER ELECTRONIC, DIGITAL OR MECHANICAL METHODS, WITHOUT THE PRIOR WRITTEN PERMISSION OF THE PUBLISHER, EXCEPT IN THE CASE OF BRIEF QUOTATIONS EMBODIED IN CRITICAL REVIEWS AS PERMITTED BY CANADIAN AND INTERNATIONAL COPYRIGHT LAWS.

ALTHOUGH THE AUTHOR AND PUBLISHER HAVE MADE EVERY EFFORT TO ENSURE THAT THE INFORMATION IN THIS BOOK WAS CORRECT AT PRESS TIME, THEY DO NOT ASSUME AND HEREBY DISCLAIM ANY LIABILITY TO ANY PARTY FOR ANY LOSS, DAMAGE, OR DISRUPTION CAUSED BY ERRORS OR OMISSIONS. SOME LINKS SUPPLIED IN THIS BOOK MAY BE AFFILIATE LINKS. AS SUCH, USING SAID LINKS MAY RESULT IN THE AUTHOR MAKING A SMALL MONETARY COMMISSION.

THE AUTHOR AND THE PUBLISHER HEREBY DISCLAIMS ALL WARRANTIES. THE INFORMATION PROVIDED TO YOU IS MADE AVAILABLE "AS IS" WITHOUT WARRANTY OF ANY KIND. YOU ASSUME THE RISK OF ANY AND ALL DAMAGE OR LOSS FROM USE OF, OR INABILITY TO USE, THE INFORMATION AND/OR SUGGESTIONS TO THE MAXIMUM EXTENT PERMITTED BY LAW, INCLUDING, BUT NOT LIMITED TO, ANY IMPLIED WARRANTIES OF SUCCESS OR EARNING POTENTIAL. ALWAYS SEEK PROFESSIONAL LEGAL AND BUSINESS ADVICE BEFORE ENDEAVORING ON ANY PROJECT THAT MAY OR MAY NOT HAVE A MONETARY IMPACT.

Table of Contents

About the Author 5
Introduction.. 9
It's Who you Know... or is it?... 16
Making a short film is not the same as writing it. 19
10 things I Learned Writing & Producing Short Films 23
    1. Talent is Easy to Find if you have this…............................... 23
    2. Wardrobe Matters.. 27
    3. Guns Need to Look Real 29
    4. Notify the Authorities... 33
    5. Pack Your Own Gear.. 36
    6. Little Things Add Up 38
    7. Don't Skimp on Extras 42
    8. It's Not A Democracy.. 44
    9. Assign Jobs (even if they're Volunteers) 55
    10. Craft Services 58
Hey, Sh!t Happens 60
The Magic Formula to Making Great Short Films 62
Bonus Exercises 63
    Finding a Story Exercise #1 – Learn Something New 65
    Finding a Story Exercise #2 – Interview................................... 68
    Finding a Story Exercise #3 – 5 Main Points in a Treatment... 72
Writing a Treatment 75
Character Development 77
    The Main Character 78
    Bringing a Character to Life 80
    Character Bio 83

Breaking Down a Scene 85
    Exercise # 1 – Breakdown a Scene you Like 85
    Exercise # 2 – Breakdown a Scene you Dislike 88
Understanding Theme 91
    Theme Exercise # 1 – What's the Theme? 93
    Theme Exercise # 2 – Think Outside the Box 94
Loglines 96
    Logline Exercise – Write Your Logline 102
That's a Wrap! 104

About the Author

Born in Toronto in 1966, Kenn Crawford grew up in the coal-mining town of Glace Bay on Cape Breton, an island off the coast of Nova Scotia, Canada.

He spent his childhood reading books and making up stories; a hobby that led to his love of writing poetry, songs, and short stories. Eventually, he began writing books and screenplays.

In 2002, he wrote a weekly newspaper column about songwriting and home recording. He appeared in *The Cape Bretoner* Magazine as the featured songwriter.

In 2016, he took his love of making up stories to the next level by writing, shooting, and directing short films.

In 2018, he won a "Canada Shorts" Director's Award of Commendation.

Over the years he has founded several businesses, including an advertising company, a computer store, and a restaurant, all of which he later sold to pursue other business ventures. He also worked as a disc jockey, ventriloquist, musician, and owned a small recording studio.

Kenn lives on Cape Breton Island with his fiancé, Margie, shooting short films and music videos, and teaching writing and filmmaking workshops. He is currently working on several new fiction and nonfiction books.

For more information about Kenn, his writing and his film work, visit his website at: www.kenncrawford.com

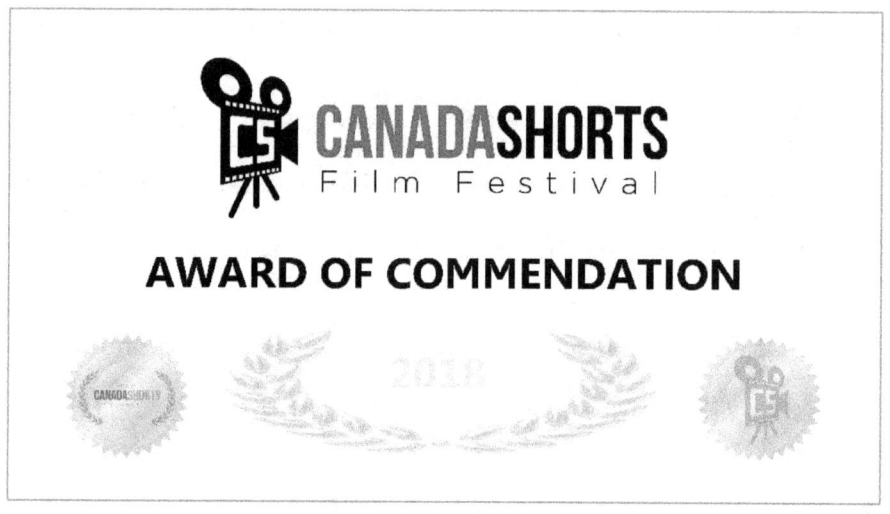

Books by Kenn

FICTION

Dead Hunt: Some Things are Better Left Dead *(zombie thriller)*

Code 900: A Derrick Stone Crime Story *(thriller)*

The Saga of Bayou Billy *(comedy)*

The Misadventures of Mallory Malo: A Ghost Story She's Dying to Tell You *(middle-grade)*

The Princess Knights *(children's story, young reader)*

NONFICTION

The Covid Chronicles: Personal Pandemic Stories from Around the World: 2020 *(true stories, memoirs, poems)*

How to Write & Publish Non-Fiction: *a Self-Publishing Guide for First-Time Writers (Self-Help, DIY)*

10 Things I Learned Shooting Short Films: *A Reality Check for First-Time Filmmakers (Self-Help, DIY)*

FILM MAKING TOOLS

The Indie Filmmaker's Shot List: Create film and video shot lists *(200 pages - 8.5" x 11")*

The Indie Filmmaker's Storyboard Book: Create storyboards for your indie film or video shoot. *(200 pages - 8.5" x 11")*

**For more information, visit:
kenncrawford.com/books**

This page intentionally left blank

Introduction

Ever since I was a little kid, I would make up stories. Most kids grow out of it, but I never did. Throughout my teens and into adulthood I would visualize entire scenes and stories as if a movie was playing in my head. I wrote some of them as short stories and books, but because I was a visual person and could see the entire story playing out in my head, I always dreamed of someday making a movie.

At first, filmmaking was just a pipe dream because video cameras, film, and the cost of developing that film was simply too expensive. But the digital revolution, namely DSLR cameras (Digital Single-Lens Reflex), put filmmaking in the hands of anyone who had the drive and passion to turn their ideas into a movie… and it was possible to do it for a modest investment that didn't include the expense of developing film, and editing video on a home computer was possible. It was time to make that movie I always wanted to make.

But where do you start when you live on an island and you don't know anyone in the filmmaking industry?

You Start with a Screenplay.

That's the first step. Nothing else matters if you don't have a story worth shooting as a properly formatted screenplay.

Ideas are a dime a dozen, but you can't shoot "ideas." You can however shoot a screenplay, which is your ideas wrote down in a way that makes sense to everyone in the filmmaking industry.

The screenplay is the roadmap of how to shoot your story.

Without a screenplay, also known as a script, directors have nothing to direct, the actors have nothing to say or do, the light department has nothing to light, the audio department has nothing to record and so on.

All films, whether it's a feature-length movie costing over a hundred million dollars or a short film costing less than a hundred bucks, they all start with the humble yet oh so important screenplay.

I studied filmmaking for years. Eventually I grew tired of just learning about filmmaking and decided to take that first, all-important step and actually make a movie. My plan was to write a short, inexpensive zombie film that I could shoot over the weekend starring my teenage daughter and her cheerleading friends.

Like most first-time writers my overactive imagination ran wild, and the story took on a life of its own…

In one scene I wrote there was a giant bear that was standing in the middle of the narrow, mountain road. A horde of zombies were approaching from the rear, but the bear was blocking the road and had no intentions on moving. So one of them leaned out of the van and offered themselves up as bait to try and coax the bear from the middle of the road. Then, when the bear moved to the side of the van, they would pull the guy in, slam the door closed, and speed away… leaving the bear and the horde of zombies in their dust.

It was a great scene, but there was just one problem…

I didn't own a bear.

I didn't know anyone that owned a bear and even if I did, there was no way I was putting my teenage daughter anywhere near that thing!

That and several other scenes I wrote looked great on paper, but I couldn't actually film them because they were simply too expensive, too dangerous, or both.

Disheartened, my screenplay for *Dead Hunt* sat for years collecting dust until I discovered author-produced podcast audiobooks. I rewrote *Dead Hunt* as a novel, and the full cast audio book version became fairly popular, but that didn't satisfy my hunger to make a movie.

Half a dozen years later I made the decision to rewrite *Dead Hunt* again as a new screenplay… only this time it was going to be a screenplay I could actually produce as a feature-length film.

Having a built-in fanbase to a popular audiobook was great, but in order to show potential cast and crew, and investors, that I could make a movie, I needed to have something to show them that I actually knew what I was doing.

So, as I was planning *Dead Hunt*, I decided to write a short film that I could shoot over a weekend to get some of that much needed hands-on experience… and to show people that I wasn't just talking the talk - I could walk the walk too.

But I was still in the same boat…

I still didn't know anyone in the industry. And when it came to thinking of a story I could shoot as a short film, my mind was drawing a blank.

Then it occurred to me that rather than trying to think of a story, I should work backwards and start with a location I knew I could get for free and use props that I already had or could borrow to help cut down on costs.

As I stood staring out my front window trying to think of a cool location that would look great on camera, the proverbial light bulb in my head went off…

I was already looking at the perfect location. A gorgeous panoramic view of the Atlantic Ocean with tall, rocky cliffs and crashing waves below. What more could a filmmaker want for a visually appealing opening scene?

With that location in mind, I started asking myself 'What if?' questions…

What if *this* happened; what if *that* happened? What if, what if, what if…

Before long I had the basic idea for a story, so I sat down to write the screenplay.

A few hours later the first draft was done. Several rewrites later the story was really taking shape.

Of course, my imagination still kept running wild, and I had to constantly remind myself not to include anything that I couldn't afford to shoot.

Props were replaced because I didn't have them or they would be too expensive to build, and the number of locations were cut back to make filming it more manageable, and I cut back on the cast to only include main actors instead of background actors.

By the time I was done cutting this and changing that, my first short film, *The Final Goodbye*, had nothing in common with my original idea, other than that opening scene of standing on the bank looking out at the Atlantic Ocean.

But that's how you write screenplays you can actually afford to shoot… by first getting your idea out of your head and on paper, and then reworking it until everything you cannot shoot or do not have access to for free has been replaced with budget-friendly props, locations, wardrobe, and so on.

Once I had a great screenplay that I could actually shoot, my next step was to find a cast and crew, but I still didn't know anyone in the filmmaking industry…

So now what do I do?

It's Who you Know... or is it?

Sometimes it's not who you know or even who your friends know, it might just be **who wants to know you.**

Before I wrote the screenplay for the short film, a few friends were helping me find affordable locations for *Dead Hunt* and pitching in where they could, but progress on the *Dead Hunt* movie was moving at a snail's pace because, as a filmmaker, I was still an unknown. In fact, I wasn't even a filmmaker because I never shot anything yet!

The heaviest website traffic I received was 75 hits a day. The audiobook version of *Dead Hunt* may have been downloaded more than 88,000 times in the first four months of its debut but getting the word out about my movie was proving to be much more difficult.

Then someone shared one of my posts, a few of their friends shared it, and within a couple of hours my website had nearly 3,200 hits! The following day it was just shy of 6,000 hits, then another 10,000 hits the following day.

My inbox was filling up with close to 500 emails from people requesting to be involved in the movie.

Dan Yakimchuk (AKA Dr. StrangeJob) was shooting a short film and asked me if I would be in his film as a background extra. I jumped at the opportunity! It was a great learning experience and I got to meet some wonderful people including the director, Michael G. MacDonald *(Legend of The Psychotic Forest Ranger.)* Mick helped me on *The Final Goodbye* as one of the camera operators, and he became an Associate Producer on *Dead Hunt,* and later starred in several of my short films.

Filmmaker Brett Holmes (*Turned, David's Girlfriend*) contacted me and later became the Director of Photography on *The Final Goodbye*. Several more people contacted me about hair and makeup, set design, wardrobe, sound, and more for *Dead Hunt*... people I could ask to help me with my short film.

My network of people interested in filmmaking was growing and I hadn't even filmed anything yet!

Darren Andrea (*The Undertaker's Wedding, La Femme Nikita, Kung Fu: The Legend Continues*) auditioned for a role in *Dead Hunt*. I discovered he was passionate about indie filmmaking, and he later starred in one of my shorts.

And it all happened because one person who I didn't even know shared one of my posts about *Dead Hunt*, and it just sort of snowballed from there. That's the power of social media.

I didn't know anyone in the filmmaking industry when I first started, but because word was spreading about *Dead Hunt*, so much so that a couple of local newspapers called to do a story on me, and because I was interviewed on CBC Radio, <u>people suddenly wanted to know me!</u>

Making a Short Film is Not the Same as Writing it.

I can say without hesitation that it was because of my experiences shooting short films that I decided to put *Dead Hunt* on the backburner and focus on shooting more shorts. I may have studied filmmaking for years, but **hands-on experience is by far the best teacher.**

Every time I step on a film set I learn something new. Despite how much I read about filmmaking, I never knew how much I didn't know until I actually started doing it. And because of that, I highly recommend that you don't shoot a feature-length film right away.

Not yet, because chances are, you're just not ready.

Sorry, but it's true.

Yes, I know you're passionate about your feature-length film.

Yes, I know how much it means to you and that you'll never give up.

I know all that and more, but guess what?

You're probably going to get overwhelmed and give up despite your passion and level of commitment because at the end of the day, it's your film... No one but you will ever be as passionate about it as you are, and you cannot make a feature film alone.

Your volunteer cast and crew may start out as passionate as you, but as the realities of filmmaking kicks in, and doing the same scene over and over again stops being fun and boredom sets in, cast and crew members will stop showing up. Problems will arise. Shortcuts will be taken... and eventually your dream will come to a screeching halt because you ran out of time, money, or both.

It's a common tale.

Yes, there are outliers who against all odds finished their feature film and it was actually pretty good, but most beginners who try to shoot a feature film first eventually give up, or their finished film is not very good because they didn't know what they were doing.

Considering how expensive a feature can get, and how time consuming it really is, it's just not worth the risk.

To avoid that almost inevitable outcome, I urge you to start with a couple of low and no-budget short films so you can learn some of the things you probably don't even realize you need to learn, such as:

- Learning how long it takes you to shoot a scene, and why it matters.
- How to direct actors.
- How to hold auditions to find the best characters and not just the best actors.
- How to have a table read, and why you shouldn't ignore them.
- How to run a film set and not let it run you.
- How to light a scene.
- How to block a scene.
- How to capture clean audio.
- Learning about inserts and cutaways.
- Learning the different types of shots and when to best use them.
- Learning when and how to use motivated camera movements.
- How to write and shoot new scenes on the fly because your original plan didn't work for whatever reason.
- Learning how to trust your team and not micromanage them.
- How to create a shot list or storyboard.

- ❖ How to make a budget – and stick to it!
- ❖ And learning how to edit a short film before you even think of taking on the daunting task of writing, shooting, and editing a feature-length film.

You're going to make mistakes, that's how we learn, so doesn't it make more sense to make those mistakes and learn from them with inexpensive shorts rather than spending a pile of time and money discovering the hard way that you're in over your head and bit off more than you can chew?

As previously mentioned, most first-time filmmakers never finish their feature because they ran out of time, money, or both. Filmmaking is not difficult per se, but it takes a lot longer and is more work than you can imagine. So why risk it with an expensive, feature-length film your first time out?

Save that epic feature film until you have more hands-on experience and a few short films under your belt so you know exactly what you're getting yourself into. That way, when you do shoot your feature, your chances of finishing it will be that much greater.

10 things I Learned Writing & Producing Short Films

1. Talent is Easy to Find if you have this…

A Great Script!

That's the long and short of it.

There are a lot of talented people out there who will jump at the chance of being in a film that has a great script. Just as you are an aspiring filmmaker, there are aspiring actors and people wanting to learn filmmaking that are willing to volunteer their time to get experience and exposure on a production.

Much to my surprise, and delight, my hometown of less than 20,000 people, and the neighboring towns and cities, has a thriving community of actors, writers, directors, camera operators, makeup artists, sound techs and more… I just never knew they existed, and not all of them are inexperienced.

I had the fortune of attracting several actors who worked on feature films and popular TV shows, and many of them volunteered to help me make my short films. And that's not counting the actors who did local theater.

You do not have to live in a big city to find people interested in filmmaking! My entire island only has around 101,000 people, and I found a lot of actors and crew members willing to get involved.

The most important thing to remember is it all starts with a great script.

Good scripts, scripts that just need a little tweaking, or that awesome idea that you think will make a great short film does not attract talent… great scripts do.

Posting to Facebook groups is a good way to find people interested in filmmaking, just make sure you list your town/city and state/province so as not to get offers from people who are not able to physically be on set.

Highschool and college drama clubs are a great place to find actors. Just remember that acting in a movie is not the same as acting in a play.

For starters, the actor does not have to project their voice as much because there will be a microphone just above their head to pick up the finer nuances of the human voice; nuances that do not work as well in a theater production. Projecting their voice too much changes the timbre and volume of their lines, and it often comes across as sounding fake and unbelievable.

The same holds true for body language…

In theater, they often use bigger gestures to show emotion and larger movements so that the people in the back can see them, but this doesn't work in film. The camera is great for picking up subtleties (that's why we use closeups) and over-emphasizing emotions or gestures will come across as bad acting despite them being a talented stage actor. It really does make a difference.

During various auditions I discovered that most stage actors are quite talented and can "switch gears" from big gestures and projecting their voice to using subtlety and minor nuances, but a small handful just couldn't "get it." No matter how many times they were directed to tone it down a little and just be natural, they just couldn't switch off their "stage actor" brain and kept "over acting" with big, bold gestures and over emphasizing subtle dialog.

Unfortunately, none of them ever landed a role in any of my short films, but the ones who could switch gears from acting on stage to acting in front of a camera appeared in several of my shorts.

The reason I am telling you this is so that you don't automatically dismiss stage actors who "over act" during auditions. Some of them don't know the difference because that's the way they were trained – for the stage. It's your job to direct them during auditions. They can't give you what you want if they don't know; you have to direct them.

If after several attempts they still keep delivering the same "over-the-top" performance, graciously thank them for their time and move on to the next audition.

Another source for finding cast and crew is your local library. You can post a notice that you are shooting a short film and you should get a few replies. It's been my experience that most actors are avid readers, and most librarians know just about everyone, especially if you live in a town or small city.

2. Wardrobe Matters

Costumes help visually establish a character, so you need to make sure you get it right.

If you're like most indie filmmakers, the costumes will be put together from your own wardrobe, items you bought at thrift stores, and mostly from your actor's own clothing. But they need to suit the character, or it could undermine the theme and tone of your film.

When I first started, my actors asked me what they should wear, and my short and sweet answer was based on technical requirements rather than being character driven, such as: don't wear all black or all white, and nothing with pinstripes or small patterns because it'll cause moiré on camera and look weird.

One of the contacts I made through *Dead Hunt*, Lyn Day, studied wardrobe for years and graciously agreed to read the script for *The Final Goodbye* and offered some amazing insight. Her two-page feedback had everything from their social standing according to their house and furniture, what the wife would be wearing during the weekday and on the weekend to allow the husband time to do everything he was doing in the script. What the husband would be wearing that made sense for his character, and so on.

It was amazing how much she read into the characters and the character's needs based off the script.

Her two-page report taught me that wardrobe, even if it's not a period piece, is not to be taken lightly because the clothes your actors are wearing does impact the overall believability of the story you are trying to tell.

3. Guns Need to Look Real

If you have a limited budget, and nearly every first-time filmmaker does, getting prop guns is not that easy and can get expensive, but with a little luck and a can-do attitude, it's not impossible.

My short film required one handgun and all I had was a pellet gun. At a distance it looked real enough, but when the actor and I did a few camera tests I quickly discovered that we had to change a lot of the blocking (where the actor physically is in the scene and what he or she is doing) because on camera, it looked like a relatively harmless pellet gun.

My friend Andrew Parland had a more realistic looking BB gun, but it was clear plastic. Andrew painted it black to make it look more realistic, but it still required the actor to hold it a certain way when filming it from different angles, and closeups did not look very realistic either. Plus, I couldn't rack the slide on either of them, so we had to work around that as well.

Then a few days before the shoot my Director of Photography said he had an airsoft gun that looked like a real gun and we could rack the slide. That meant no more specialized blocking or framing required and I could shoot the scene the way I originally envisioned and wrote it. That was, until we arrived on set and he couldn't find the magazine for his gun.

Some last-minute blocking changes were needed, and for the most part it worked but in some scenes people may notice that the magazine is missing.

Welcome to low budget filmmaking.

A Word about Guns:

It's always best to have someone on set who knows guns and is in charge of making sure they are used responsibly. This person is called a gun wrangler or an armorer.

On one of my short films, we were filming on a beach and the gun wrangler was my friend Derrick Roberts, who was also an ex-cop.

When one of the actors was goofing around during a break and pointed the prop rifle at someone on the other end of the beach, Derrick was super quick to put a stop to it. He informed the actor (and everyone else on set) that it doesn't matter if the gun is fake, the person the actor was pointing the rifle at doesn't know that, and that person only needs to *feel* threatened and could have pressed charges.

It's also worth noting that actors have a tendency to hold guns with their finger on the trigger. People who know and use real guns NEVER do that!

In *The Final Goodbye*, the actor racked the slide twice. The first time it looked and sounded cool, but the second time meant that in the real world, he would have ejected an unused round. Real gun owners don't do that either.

Oh, and the part with the bullets that you slide into the handgun or rifle is called a magazine, not a clip. I've watched countless movies or read books when the character called it a clip.

If you're going to have weapons in your film, make sure you get the terminology right, which is why it's always a good idea to have someone who understands weapons read your script, because they will pick up on those little mistakes and help you fix them to make your film look and sound that much more realistic.

Last but not least, <u>Never Ever Use Real Guns</u>.

Yes, real guns without ammo are relatively harmless, but if someone puts a real bullet in it (for whatever reason) or they thought it wasn't loaded but there was still a round in the chamber, someone could be seriously hurt or killed.

While it is true that real guns can have the firing pin removed so that they don't fire, prop weapons are by far the safest. Not to mention, in some places it is illegal to use a real weapon on a film set even if it is not loaded.

It's just not worth the risk.

4. Notify the Authorities

If you are using any type of prop weapons (from knives to guns or even just hand-to-hand fight scenes) you should always notify the authorities, especially if you will be shooting in a location where there's a chance someone might see you because you run the risk of having them call the police.

Nothing will shut your production down faster than flashing lights and the local police showing up with their very real guns drawn.

I forgot to do this on my first short film but thankfully we didn't have any issues. Someone did see us but luckily, we saw him first, so we had time to explain that we we're shooting a movie and the gun wasn't real.

You may think you are out of the public's view when filming indoors, but if someone walks by a window and sees your actor tied up with another actor pointing a gun at them, they may not know it is a movie and call the police on you.

It's just not worth the risk.

When we were filming *The Rose*, we notified the police and explained what we were doing. They thanked us for letting them know and asked us to call them again on the day we were filming to remind them so they could *"keep it on their radar"* in case someone saw us and called it in.

We live in a small town so it didn't cost us anything to get permission from the police and we didn't even need a permit, but the cost of not notifying them could have been much, much higher.

It's worth mentioning that before I hand an actor a prop weapon, I remind them that it is fake and then point the gun at the ground and pull the trigger a couple of times to show them that it doesn't fire.

They are then reminded that when we wrap a scene or go on breaks, all guns are to be returned to the gun wrangler for safe keeping.

Then, when filming resumes, we go through the whole process again of pointing it at the ground and pulling the trigger so they always know that no one is ever in any danger.

For the web series we were filming, the character the young actress was playing carried a knife. Before I let her touch the knife, I showed her and her mother that the knife was in fact dull by running it across my own arm. I then handed it to the mother, handle first, and allowed her to inspect it before giving it to her daughter.

Safety should ALWAYS be first and foremost on every film set.

In may sound kinda silly taking all these extra precautions but trust me, the very last thing you ever want is for someone to be hurt on one of your film shoots.

As I have mentioned several times already, it's just not worth the risk.

5. Pack Your Own Gear

When the big day comes to start filming, you'll have more gear than you can imagine. There's the camera, tripod, all the props, costumes, lighting and light stands, microphones and boom poles, cables, extension cords, power bars, reflectors, rolls of gaffer tape, a first aid kit, food and water for everyone… the list seems endless.

If you're moving to a second location mid-shoot you need to resist the urge to let someone else help you pack unless that person was designated ahead of time and knows where everything goes.

When I arrived at our first location, my daughter's house, I had the bag for the camera and lenses, two duffle bags of cables, extension cords and lighting gear, a rolling suitcase with tripods and stands, a metal briefcase (for my laptop) that was also used as a prop, another laptop case for smaller items like batteries, extra memory cards, pens, paper, etc., and another case with my audio interface, the clapper board, and microphones.

We didn't need everything for the second location, a graveyard, so there was no need to take the lights and stands, so I left the stuff we didn't need at my daughter's house to save a bit of time tearing down and packing.

But when we arrived at the second location, items I needed were nowhere to be found because someone packed it in one of the cases that I was leaving behind.

To avoid this, pack the gear yourself or at the very least, have someone designated to help you pack who knows where everything belongs. Create a checklist of everything you'll need (gear, props, wardrobe, etc.) for each location, then double check it before you head out.

It may seem like you are holding everyone up, but the delays will be much longer if you have to go back and get something.

Plus, it makes you look unprofessional when you don't have a piece of gear, a prop, or anything else that is needed to film the scene.

6. Little Things Add Up

Whatever your budget is, double it. Anyone who tells you they made a film for zero dollars is either lying or naive. Did they not even buy their cast and crew a cup of coffee or offer them a bottle of water? They must have printed off copies of the script, created a storyboard or printed a shot list.

Most first-time filmmakers will estimate the obvious things like costumes, props, weapons, and so on, but it's the little things you weren't expecting that'll eat through your budget quicker than you can say, *"Where'd all the money go?"*

I wrote my first short film, *The Final Goodbye,* to be shot on a budget of zero dollars by having all volunteers and only using props, wardrobe, and locations that I could get for free.

When all was said and done, my zero-dollar short film cost one hundred and twenty dollars.

The chandelier over the table had burnt out lightbulbs that needed to be replaced, paper and ink was needed to print scripts, gas to drive to and from the locations, and I supplied coffee, water, juice and snacks on the days that we filmed.

All movies cost <u>something</u> to make, even all-volunteer short films.

For your first couple of ultra-low-budget shoots, think of everything that you will need, and don't forget to include gas to travel back and forth to the location, paper and ink to print extra copies of the script, spare batteries, extra memory cards, food and drink for everyone.

Then double that amount.

If you think it'll cost fifty dollars, budget for one hundred to cover all those little things you forgot to add or didn't know about, like bags of ice or ice packs and a cooler (Esky) if you're going to be shooting outdoors to keep the bottled water cold and to prevent the food from spoiling in the heat of summer.

As you create more films, some of those costs can be excluded (you'll have enough memory cards and camera batteries by then) but other costs are reoccurring such as craft services (food and drink), paper and ink for scripts, gas and so on.

Eventually you'll have a system down where you only have to add an extra 20-30% to your budget for incidentals instead of doubling your budget.

When your budget is in the thousands of dollars, you need to have a detailed budget created or you could end up maxing out your credit card. And you should have a couple of less expensive shorts under your belt before you even consider shooting anything that's going to cost several thousands of dollars.

Once you have a budget set you must have the self-discipline to never spend a penny beyond the budget, because the minute you open your wallet or pull out your credit card, the costs will spiral out of control, especially when you're at the point of having paid actors and crew.

Unless you are independently wealthy, you do not have a money hose to wash away problems, so you must solve them creatively rather than throwing money at it.

You may think a few extra bucks here or there doesn't really matter and you would be right… if this is the only film you will ever make. But if you plan on making more, and just about every first-time filmmaker gets bitten by the filmmaking bug and can't wait to do it again, the last habit you want to develop is trying to wash problems away with a money hose.

Create a budget and stick to it!

Gone are the days of having random pages of shots and notes scattered everywhere!

With **The Indie Filmmaker's Shot List** everything is in one place - indexed and organized for multiple projects in a professional looking book.

Eliminates the need to keep printing pages and pages of blank templates for every film shoot!

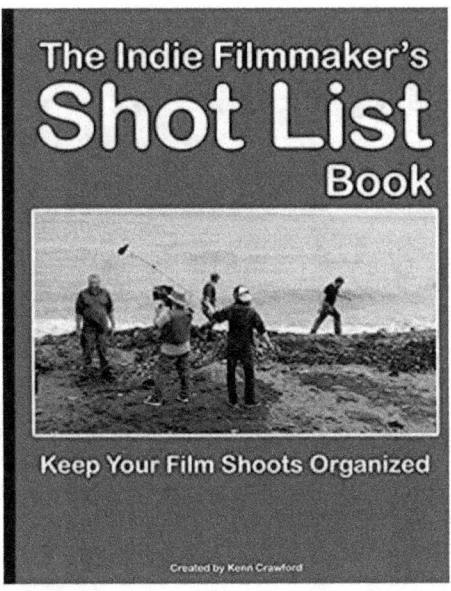

What is a Shot List and Why is it Important?

A shot list maps out exactly what shots will occur for each scene of your film.

A shot list not only gives your film shoot a sense of direction and prepares your crew so they know what to expect for each setup in the scene, but it helps you organize your thoughts before filming begins, and helps you prepare a shooting schedule.

Shot lists go hand in hand as part of the pre-production process.

Order your copy today by visiting
https://kenncrawford.com/shotlist

7. Don't Skimp on Extras (and I don't mean background actors)

Your goal should be to spend as little money as possible to shoot your short film, but some costs are unavoidable.

You can never have too many batteries or memory cards so stock up. There's nothing more annoying, or makes you look like an unprepared amateur, than running out of power or memory halfway through your shoot.

During both days of shooting *The Final Goodbye* the camera batteries went dead. That was to be expected, but on the first day he didn't bring his charger. Luckily, we had a second camera that was fully charged so we were able to keep shooting.

Remember: Shooting still images on a DSLR is not the same as shooting video…

When shooting a movie you spend a lot of time setting up and framing the shots, checking and rechecking the focus and exposure, blocking and rehearsing the scene, shooting the scene, shooting retakes, and reviewing the footage… and they all suck the life out of your batteries.

Invest in spares for your camera, several fast memory cards, and stock up on AA and AAA batteries for those "just in case" moments, like when the batteries in the audio recorder go dead. That happened on the second day of our shoot, but because I was prepared and had spares, it wasn't a problem.

Note: I mentioned in the title of this section that I wasn't referring to background extras. For your first couple of shorts, it's best to stick to just the main actors (those who have dialog) and resist the temptation to have background extras.

While it is true that having background actors does increase the production value of your final film, background actors, just like your main actors, need to be directed. You can't expect them to know what to do.

Background actors need to be blocked too, and then you need to make sure they repeated their movements EXACTLY the same way for every take or else you won't be able to edit the footage together.

It's best to get a few shorts under your belt with just the main actors before you increase your workload by adding more moving parts to the production by including background extras.

8. It's Not A Democracy

There's a chance that someone in your cast and crew has an idea for a shot that might be better than what you had planned. For this to work, they have to be comfortable telling you and you have to be open to new ideas, but at the end of the day, **it is your film**, and you have the final say.

Scratch that... **You have the ONLY say!**

If you want the opening shot to be of the actor reading a book but everyone on set loves the idea of opening with a dream sequence and then cut to him asleep holding the book, does it matter that you are out voted?

No… because there is no vote!

Filmmaking is a team sport but it's not a democracy.

Side note: Don't write a *"waking up from a dream"* scene. That cliché opening, as well as *"it was all a dream"* ending, have been done so many times that audiences really dislike them. Most people hate the *"it was all a dream"* endings because they invested their time and energy to watch your film and they got shortchanged with a cliché, unoriginal ending.

Always remember that as the director you shoot your vision…

If someone on your set insists that their ideas are better, even if they have more experience than you, it doesn't matter what they want. They can always make their own film if they insist on using their ideas because when they are on your set, they shoot *your* vision, not their interpretation of it.

For my first short film, **The Final Goodbye,** I wanted to open a certain scene with a closeup of a newspaper article and then slide the camera to the left to reveal the actor reading the paper. The DP (Director of Photography) wanted to shoot it differently. Being open to new ideas I let him try it his way because his idea would have looked great, but it was a tricky shot to pull off because it required a dolly, a tilt, and to rack focus all at the same time (while using a slider that had seen better days.)

We took so long trying to get that one shot that I eventually said he could have one more crack at it and then we move on to the next scene. He didn't get the shot and we moved on… but I never got the shot that I originally wanted.

To me, that opening shot was important because the newspaper article was one that was done on me and my upcoming feature film, *Dead Hunt*. But because he didn't get the shot he was trying to get, and I didn't insist on getting my shot first, none of the shots I did have clearly showed the newspaper article.

And that's just for a relatively unimportant "Easter egg" shot, it could have been a lot worse…

If you don't get the shot you want first, you could even end up not having the shot at all, which means during the edit you'll have to find a way to tell the story without that important shot. If you can't do that, you have to call everyone back and reshoot the scene.

Believe me, your cast and crew will not like being called back again and again to shoot one scene because you didn't get what you wanted. And even if they do agree to reshoot it, you'll be hard pressed to get them to help you on future projects because they'll know you don't know what you're doing, and you could be wasting their time… again.

If someone has an idea that's different than yours and you like it, get the shot you originally planned first before you start experimenting, and be mindful that you are not wasting your cast and crew's time because things can get boring for them very fast watching you try to get that one perfect shot over and over again.

If the shots require a lot of setup time, decide which one you want the most and go with that one. It doesn't matter if it's your idea or someone else's, it's still *your* film so pick the one that *you* want and go for it.

IMPORTANT:

It's worth noting that once I had a couple of short films under my belt, I realized that a lot of time was wasted "explaining" why I wanted to shoot the scene a certain way instead of using their idea.

Mostly it was because I wasn't just shooting a scene, I was shooting part of a bigger picture…

Things I had planned for future scenes wouldn't work as well if I changed something in an earlier scene, which means future shots or scenes will have to be changed too which slows the production down even more. This is something the "I have a great idea" people didn't realize or didn't take into consideration because they were only thinking about that one scene or one shot, and not how it affected future scenes or shots.

Filmmaking really is a puzzle, and you shoot it one piece at a time!

I also noticed that when you're on a low-budget indie film set using all volunteers, suddenly every other person thinks they are a "director" and has great ideas on how you should shoot your film… and they're more than happy to tell you!

Being open to everyone's ideas is good in one way because sometimes their ideas really are better than yours, but it can really slow the production down because while they are telling you their great idea, or you're explaining why their idea won't work, everyone else is just standing around getting bored.

To avoid these unnecessary delays, I eventually had to create a new rule:

"If anyone has any questions or ideas, I don't want to hear them."

I then explain that I really am open to ideas, but they need to tell the 1st AD (First Assistant Director) and not me because I have too many things going on in my head at any given time, and I can't keep track of everything if I am being constantly interrupted. I explain this in a polite and friendly way during a brief meeting at the beginning of the shoot so as not to come off as pretentious or rude.

They mean well, and they really are trying to help you make the best film possible, but most of them do not realize just how many different things a director is focused on and trying to keep track of, especially if they are also the camera operator, because now they are doing two full time jobs at once.

Constantly hearing ideas and answering questions means eventually I'll forget something important. To avoid that, I ask them to bring their questions and ideas to the 1st AD rather than bringing them directly to me.

All of my shoots have a 1st AD, which is someone I trust who not only knows exactly what I want, but they can answer most questions on my behalf so I can focus on my job as the director slash camera operator.

Everyone is reminded that the 1st AD runs the set and anything they say is the same as hearing it directly from me.

Trust me, a 1st AD will save your sanity and your film, because being constantly interrupted or confused during the shoot sucks the fun out of filmmaking.

It's worth noting however that before every shoot I try to have at least one table read. A table read is basically what it sounds like… the actors, as well as the director, the 1st AD, and any key production personnel, sit around a table and the actors read the script.

A table read helps you find potential problems, whether it's a line of dialog that doesn't sound nearly as good as you thought it would when you hear someone else say it, or the actor feels that something they are saying or doing in the scene would be out of character for them.

It is during the table read that I am the most open to ideas, because things can be easily changed. It's during the actual filming when I am less open to ideas because by then, the screenplay has been "locked" (it's the version that everyone has memorized, and the other departments are using as a blueprint for what they should be doing) and making changes once the camera starts rolling means everyone else has to be constantly updated of any changes so they can prepare for it.

It's a lot easier to listen to ideas and answer questions during the table read because I am mainly focusing on how the actors are delivering their lines… on set I am focusing on that and a million other things, and by then I created a shot list based on everything we discussed during the table read.

IMPORTANT:

When you first start shooting you will most likely feel both exuberant and painfully nervous. You will start to second-guess yourself, and if someone on set who has more experience than you mentions an idea, you're going to want to agree with them so as not to "make waves" and cause problems. The other fear that will be constantly nagging at you is the fear of pissing off your volunteers because you're afraid if they get mad and walk off set, the whole film shoot falls apart and the only choices you have left is to recast it and start over, or just let the project die.

Neither one sounds very appealing, so you have a tendency to go out of your way trying to please everyone, but here's the thing…

It is your shoot. Not theirs. Just because they are not getting paid doesn't mean they can be unprofessional. Professional is an attitude, not a paycheck. If they are willing to walk away because they're not getting paid and you won't use their ideas, that reflects more on them than you. It's best to let them walk away, recast it, and shoot it another day.

Yes, it'll be frustrating, and some money will be wasted, but once you give in to one actor (or crew member) you create a precedent for everyone else.

For a web series I was shooting, one of the actors was habitually late. But because he was an experienced actor, and because I didn't have enough courage to demand he be on time out of fear he would walk away and we'd have to start from scratch, he continued to be late for every shoot. In a very short time, other cast and crew started showing up late. They figured there was no point being on time because so-and-so is always late anyway so what's the point?

And they were right. They had no reason to be on time, and it didn't take long for everything to unravel and fall apart. But here's the thing... It wasn't that actor's fault...

It was mine.

Because I wouldn't stand up to anyone out of fear that they would quit, the rest of the cast and crew lost respect for me as the director. Suddenly they stopped listening to me and some even went to that actor for confirmation when I said something because to them, that actor was in control, not me.

I have no one to blame for that except myself.

I have months of footage that will never see the light of day because eventually I cancelled the entire project. I didn't have enough coverage to edit a story out of the footage I did have, and most of what I did have wasn't what I wanted anyway because I let the set run me instead of me running the set.

It was a painful and disheartening lesson to spend an entire summer and a lot of money shooting a web series with nothing to show for it.

Since then, I realized my mistake and now I take control of my sets. If a problem starts to arise, I nip in in the bud right away so it doesn't balloon into a bigger problem. I run my set; it doesn't run me.

I've learned that actors who won't take directions during an audition will not take them during the shoot either.

And yes, I had actors argue with me during auditions that how I wanted them to play the character was not how they saw the character and kept performing it their way. What they didn't know was I purposefully asked them to play it wrong to see if they would follow directions even if they disagreed with those directions. Those who didn't follow my directions fell into two categories…

    1 – they didn't know how to follow directions.

    2 – they refuse to follow directions.

Both will be a nightmare and a headache on set, so I always throw actors a "curveball" during auditions to see if they can in fact take and follow directions.

And remember, filmmaking is not a democracy. No one has any "say" on your film set but you… even if some of those people have more experience than you. Yes, its great to learn from those who have more experience, but at the end of the day, it's still your shoot. Follow your gut and stick to your guns so your film set doesn't run you.

9. Assign Jobs (even if they're Volunteers)

If you have more actors than crew, you probably need more crew. There is so much happening at once during a shoot that it's impossible to give everything your full attention. If you're like me, and most indie filmmakers are, you are writing, producing, directing, filming, and editing the movie yourself.

I'm a published songwriter, author, musician, audio editor, and an avid photographer, so you might be thinking I'd be the last person who would require a lot of help because I already have most of the bases covered and the necessary skill set to do it...

If you thought that you would be wrong.

The more you can do, the more you *want* to do, and the less you actually get done because you can only focus on so many aspects of filmmaking at once before you start missing things and making mistakes.

Running a multi-cam shoot with a small crew for my first short film meant I was checking both cameras and running the sound recorder, all while trying to make sure we followed the shot list and making sure we got enough coverage and inserts.

As if that wasn't enough, I still had to watch the performance to make sure the actor delivered what I wanted because I was the Director after all.

Things slowly spiraled out of control - shots were slated wrong, I forgot to check the audio levels, some of the setups took too long because I was preoccupied trying to solve or avoid other issues, and then when it started to rain, we had to do some one-take-wonders just to get it completed. Needless to say, I didn't get all the coverage or shots that I wanted, and editing it proved to be equally as hellish trying to sort through everything.

If you only want to direct, you need to make sure you have one person responsible for the camera (who is usually responsible for lighting the scene too), another for sound, a script supervisor to make sure you get everything, a 1st AD to run the set for you and keep everyone in line, and someone to slate the shots so you can focus mainly on directing.

Having everyone helping out where they can and doing what needs to be done sounds great in theory, but in practice it often results in mistakes because somebody thought somebody else was taking care of it.

I've ran several businesses, including a restaurant, so I know from experience that the attitude of *"We'll all chip in and do whatever needs to be done"* rarely works, and if it does it's usually when things are slow. On busy days, having a designated person responsible for each piece of the puzzle is the only way to get through the day with the least number of mistakes. And film shoots are always "busy days" because there is so much going on at any given time.

On a low budget film with a small crew, it's not uncommon for some crew members to be pulling double and triple duties, but make sure those duties do not overlap because that's when *"I thought so-and-so was doing that"* mistakes start to happen.

Having one person for each task is great in theory, until you have to feed everyone during breaks, and that can get quite expensive. You need to find a happy medium of having enough crew to help you shoot your film but not so many that they are mostly standing around bored, or craft services (food) eats up too much of your small budget.

As you shoot more and more projects, you'll start to build a great team who you know has your back and will help you get the job done.

10. Craft Services

"A Fed Cast and Crew is a Happy Cast and Crew."

Repeat that phrase until it's drilled into your head so that you never forget it.

Getting people excited and volunteering to help with your film project is not that difficult if you have a great script. But that excitement quickly wears off when their bellies are growling, and boredom makes people hungry when they are standing around waiting for their scene or waiting to do their job as a crew member.

Set-up times, blocking, re-takes, and breaks in general mean people are just standing around. Having a coffee or something to snack on goes a long way to keep morale high.

I didn't have a lot of money for my short films, but I always made sure I at least had plenty of coffee, tea, bottled water, juice, and donuts for everyone.

The short film I was asked to be an extra in had various types of sandwiches, a tray of cold meats, a tray of fruit, and a variety of other snacks like donuts for everyone involved, including coffee, tea, water, and juice.

It may not seem like much, but the simple gesture of making sure your cast and crew at least have coffee, water and something to snack on tells your cast and crew that you appreciate everything they are doing for you.

Always remember: **Without them, your screenplay will never get off the written page!**

Craft services should always be one of your top priorities when it comes to filmmaking, especially when it comes to volunteers, so make sure that's the first item in your budget.

Hey, Sh!t Happens

It doesn't matter how much you try to plan for everything, something you would never expect in a million years will magically happen just to make filming your project something you will never forget.

Here are just a few of the things that went wrong when filming my very first short film: *The Final Goodbye:*

- Our hair and makeup person couldn't make it due to an emergency.
- The night before the shoot a crew member slipped and spent the night at the hospital with a cracked rib.
- The owner of the camera I borrowed dropped and broke their main camera and had to get their other one back from me because they had a wedding to shoot.
- During the shoot, one of the actors received a phone call about a death in the family, so they obviously had to leave.
- The person who said they would play the mother got laryngitis the day before the shoot.
- The second person who said they would fill in and play the mother ended up going to the hospital because her husband was in an industrial accident.
- The child for the flashback scene with the mother would not cooperate (no surprise there because children are difficult to work with, especially very young children) but he slipped and cut his head and needed several

- stitches a few days before the shoot, so we had to make sure we only shot him from an angle that didn't show the bandage.

- His mother broke her arm and had to wear a cast during the scene. *I was beginning to think that scene was cursed.*

- The first day of the shoot we were rained out, and then we were snowed out on the same day. We were rained out the following two weekends, and it started to rain before we wrapped up shooting (hence those few one-take wonders just to get the film finished.)

- One of the actors had to be out of town for three weeks which delayed the shooting even more.

There's no way you can prepare for everything. You can have contingency plans to try and cover as many bases as possible, but some days things just go wrong. Your project is not cursed nor is any of it a sign to give up…

It's called filmmaking!

Things go wrong on a film shoot ALL THE TIME.

All you can do is deal with each one as it happens and keep pushing forward. Your sense of accomplishment for you, your cast, and your crew will be that much greater because you still created your film in spite of everything that went wrong.

The Magic Formula to Making Great Short Films

Step 1: Write a great screenplay.

Step 2: Shoot and edit it.

Step 3: Repeat steps 1 and 2.

That's it, that's the big secret! The magic formula to making great short films is repetition… The more you do it, the better you will become.

There is only so much you can learn from a book or an online course because at the end of the day, experience is the best teacher, and the only way you can get that is to get out there and shoot your films!

Maybe the first couple won't be that great, but you'll learn from them, make adjustments, and each film will be better than the last.

I've been at this a while and I still learn something new every time I step on a film set.

Experience is the only teacher that matters… so write your screenplays, shoot your films, and become the filmmaker you always dreamed of becoming.

Bonus Exercises

Included with this book are several of the exercises that I use when teaching writing and filmmaking workshops. I have included them here to help you on your quest to becoming a better screenwriter and better filmmaker.

If you're reading the paperback version of this book, I suggest you write these exercises on sheets of lined paper rather than writing in the book itself because these exercises can and should be used for future screenplays.

Obviously, you cannot write in the ebook version, but Kindle's do allow you to take notes. Even though you will be writing out these exercises on paper, you should highlight these exercises in your Kindle so you can quickly find them again when you want to work on new screenplays and develop new characters.

Storyboards are an effective way to quickly tell a story.

Storyboards are a sequence of drawings that represent how you plan to shoot your movie or video project.

Storyboards cover all the major shots, angles, and action of your film, and is a very important part of the pre-production process because it clearly conveys how your story will flow.

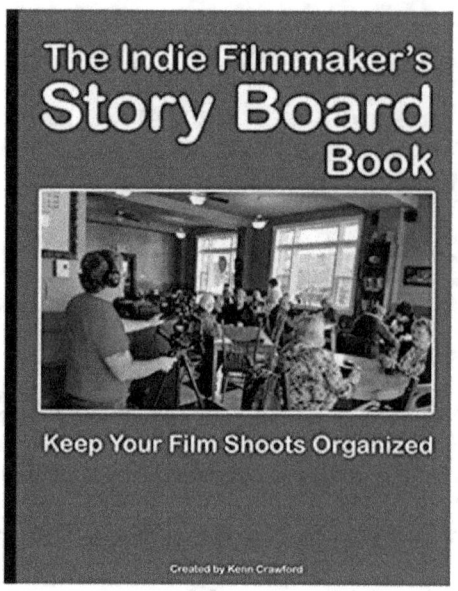

During pre-production, storyboards allow you to tell the story visually. Plus, they help you keep track of the shots you want to get when you're on set shooting the raw footage.

Storyboards often contain technical notes, markups to show camera movement, and lines of dialogue. The drawings can be anything from quick, stick-figure doodles to detailed drawings – both ensure that your entire team is on the same page when it comes time to shoot your film.

The Indie Filmmaker's Storyboard Book helps you stay organized by keeping all your drawings in one place, in a professional-looking book, and allows you to focus on the panels you need to shoot a great film rather than trying to create and print pages and pages of templates.

4 panels per page with lines below each panel to write production notes or dialog.

Order your copy today by visiting: https://kenncrawford.com/storyboard

Finding a Story Exercise #1 – Learn Something New

Researching something you have no knowledge of can be useful when looking for a story idea or something to include to add extra depth to the character and to the story.

For Example: The topic could be computer programming. The story around the topic could be about a computer virus infecting the city's power grid, hackers taking over the subway system, or writing a computer virus to take control of an alien ship.

By doing a little research into computer programming and hacking to learn new facts, you would discover that showing the classic, pre-Windows, flashing green MS-DOS prompt is not only cliché, but also unrealistic in modern-day computer programming. How many times have you watched a movie where the hacker only had to type a few words in MS-DOS like *run password crack* and seconds later the hacker magically has full access to the entire system?

That's not the way it works. Show your audience a different view with more modern programming languages such as Kali Linux, and your hacker is running Bash, Ruby or Python shells to gain access.

In a feature-length film, the subject could be a subplot or for character building, but in a short film you do not have time for subplots so the subject would be a part of the main story.

Pick a subject and list five facts about that topic:

Subject: _____

1. _____

2. _____

3. _____

4. _____

5. _____

Pick one of those facts and write how you can include it in a story.

How does this fact work for or against your main character?

Is it something they have to learn?

What would be the consequence of not knowing the fact?

Remember that short films do not have a lot of time for character development, so you have to include this information without using long exposition. How can you work it into your film without giving your audience an info dump?

Using the previous questions as a guide, write how you can use one of the facts from your list in a story in a new, creative way:

_____
_____
_____
_____
_____
_____
_____
_____
_____
_____

Finding a Story Exercise #2 – Interview

Everyone has a story to tell. For this exercise ask a friend or relative for permission to interview them about their life. Keep in mind that an older person will usually have more stories to tell because they had more life experiences to draw from.

Tip 1: Interview your subject as a journalist. Ask detailed, probing questions and take copious notes. Record the interview if possible.

Tip 2: Use an audio recorder, such as your cellphone, instead of a video camera. People will be less apprehensive about an unobtrusive audio recorder sitting on the table than a video camera stuck in their face. They'll probably be a little apprehensive at first, just ignore the recorder and talk to them; eventually they'll forget about the recorder too and really start to open up.

Don't get hung up on your list of questions. The key is to be an active listener. If they say something interesting, ask them follow-up questions to explain what they mean in more detail. People love to talk about their experiences… the key is to let them!

Example: When I was in high school, a classmate and I had to do a report on World War II. Rather than simply looking up the same information that everyone else had access to, we decided to interview my grandfather, a WWII vet.

Not only did he give us more than enough material for the school project, I had plenty of material I could use for several stories that people would find interesting.

I later "interviewed" my grandfather again because I was genuinely interested in what he went through during the war. Some of those stories would make the hairs on the back of your neck stand up! Someday I will write a short film and incorporate his harrowing ordeals into that screenplay.

Review the recording and your notes and find those snippets that could be expanded on as a story. If the interview gives you enough ideas for several stories, remember that your primary goal is to find that one great idea worth writing about because it's a story that needs to be told.

Write 1 to 5 ideas for a story based on the interview.

Interviewee's Name: _____

Story Ideas:

1. _____
   _____
   _____
   _____
   _____
   _____

2. _____
   _____
   _____
   _____
   _____
   _____

3. _____
   _____
   _____
   _____
   _____

4. _____
_____
_____
_____
_____

5. _____
_____
_____
_____
_____

Finding a Story Exercise #3 – 5 Main Points in a Treatment

A treatment is basically a summary of what happens in a story but without dialogue (unless it's a key line needed to move the story forward.) Writing a treatment can help you see the direction the story is taking before you commit to writing the screenplay.

For this exercise, fill in the working title and the five main points for your story idea:

> Note: Don't get hung up on trying to come up with the "Perfect Title" because you can always change it later. Just give it a working title that makes sense for the idea and move on to the first main point.

Working Title:

1 - A logline is one or two sentences that explains what the story is about. We'll cover loglines in more detail later in thebook, for now, just write a brief summary.

Logline:

2 - The setup is a little about the background and some build-up.

The Setup: _____

_____

_____

3 - The hook is what makes your story different and original.

The Hook: _____

_____

_____

4 - The resolution is how the story ends. Does the protagonist achieve their goal?

The Resolution: _____

_____

_____

5 - What obstacles will the protagonist face? Keep in mind that a short film is typically about one problem (obstacle) that the protagonist has to face but writing down several obstacles gives you the opportunity to explore your story idea a little deeper and find the best idea to turn into a short film.

Obstacles:

Writing a Treatment

A screenplay treatment in its most basic form is simply the plot of your story written down in free-form prose in a *"This happens then this happens then this happens"* play-by-play format of what happens in your story.

Using the information on the previous pages to guide you, name your characters and write a few paragraphs about what happens in your story. Don't worry about dialog unless it's a key line.

Keep in mind that just like the working title, don't get hung up on finding the perfect name or names for your characters because you can always change them later.

Treatment:

_____
_____
_____
_____
_____
_____
_____
_____ (continued next page)

Character Development

Many stories and films are character driven; this means that the character has an interesting personality and their way of perceiving and interacting with the people and things around them are what drives the story forward. This exercise will help you develop your main character, as well as the other characters in your story.

Remember that short films do not have time to fully develop the characters with big character arcs because shorts are typically about a single problem the character needs to solve. But doing these exercises will help you define your character even though most of it will not make it into the short film itself.

The Main Character

What is your main character's dramatic need? In other words, what does the character want to win/gain/get/achieve? What is their motivation? Define their dramatic need in a sentence or two.

_____
_____
_____
_____
_____

What is your character's Point of View? How do they see the world and the people around them? Are they an optimist, a pessimist, a cynic, a dreamer? Define their point of view in a sentence or two.

_____
_____
_____
_____
_____

Change is what dramatic writing is all about. Seeing how a character changes allows the audience to connect with and be emotionally invested in that character. Write a few sentences to describe how your character changes (their character arc) over the course of your story

_____
_____
_____
_____
_____
_____

Bringing a Character to Life

You never want to write flat, cookie-cutter characters. Writing interesting, three-dimensional characters is how you get your audience to relate to your characters and to your story because people do not get emotionally invested in clichés.

One of the best ways to make your characters more realistic is to understand their history.

When your character has a past it defines them as an individual, and it influences the choices they make in your story because of their past experiences.

I usually caution new writers that developing a rich biography runs the risk of falling in love with that biography, and you may want to include it in your screenplay even if it has nothing to do with the story you're supposed to be telling. That being said, having a biography can help you create better, more realistic characters, so I have included one for you to fill out.

For this exercise, write a brief biography of your character. Include their likes, dislikes, and any dramatic experience they may have had starting from their birth up to the point at which we meet them in your story.

I mentioned "from birth" but you do not need to include every detail. This exercise is only a brief biography, so just touch on a few likes and dislikes and list a few dramatic experiences they may have had that's relevant to your story.

For example: If you write in the biography that your character was left behind a dumpster as a baby and then raised by a group of street kids who barely knew how to take care of themselves, but your actual story is about an undercover cop who has his cover blown during a drug buy, what does that part of his biography have to do with the actual story?

Nothing.

But because you fell in love with that part of the biography, you may want to "force it" into the story by having the character talk about his upbringing, even though it has nothing to do with the actual story you're supposed to be telling, which creates a lot of unnecessary exposition of the character talking about his feelings… exposition that will bore your audience.

You told them it was about an undercover cop having his cover blown during a drug buy, so tell them that story and don't "force" irrelevant biography into it just because you like it.

Remember that the other characters in your story should have a dramatic need as well, including your antagonist. They can't simply be there to try and stop the protagonist from achieving their goal, **the antagonist must have a reason for wanting to stop them**.

This will help keep you from writing flat, cookie-cutter characters that nobody really likes because they're too predictable and boring.

Character Bio

(Character Bio, continued)

Breaking Down a Scene

Exercise # 1 – Breakdown a Scene you Like

For this exercise you're going to look at a scene from your favorite movie and break the scene down. This exercise is designed to breakdown a single scene, not the entire movie.

By understanding what you like about films will help your writing because you'll have a better idea of what works and doesn't work for you.

It's best to ignore the acting for this exercise. I've watched some great stories that had less than stellar acting, but the story carried the film and kept it interesting despite the stiff acting.

Title of a film I like: _____

What happens in the scene?

_____
_____
_____
_____
_____

Is the intention of the scene to move the plot forward or is it used for character development? What aspects of the scene brought you to that conclusion?

_____
_____
_____
_____
_____
_____
_____

What stands out the most in the scene?

_____
_____
_____
_____
_____
_____
_____
_____
_____
_____

Does the dialogue sound natural and realistic, or forced and unrealistic? What aspects of the dialogue brought you to that conclusion?

_____
_____
_____
_____
_____
_____
_____

What would you do differently if you were directing the scene?

_____
_____
_____
_____
_____
_____
_____
_____

Exercise # 2 – Breakdown a Scene you Dislike

For this exercise you're going to look at a scene from a movie you do not like and break the scene down.

Just like the previous exercise, this is designed to breakdown a single scene and not the entire movie.

By understanding what you dislike about the movie it'll help you improve your writing because you'll have a better idea of what doesn't work as far as you are concerned.

Title of a film I dislike: _____

What happens in the scene?

_____
_____
_____
_____
_____
_____
_____
_____
_____

Is the intention of the scene to move the plot forward or is it used for character development? What aspects of the scene brought you to that conclusion?

_____
_____
_____
_____
_____
_____
_____

What stands out the most in the scene?

_____
_____
_____
_____
_____
_____
_____
_____

Does the dialogue sound natural and realistic, or forced and unrealistic? What aspects of the dialogue brought you to that conclusion?

_____
_____
_____
_____
_____
_____
_____
_____

What would you do differently if you were directing the scene?

_____
_____
_____
_____
_____
_____
_____
_____
_____

Understanding Theme

Your story's theme is what your story is really about. A love story is not just about two people finding love - it could be about whether or not they can respect each other for who they are, it could be about forgiveness, it could be about trust, it could be about surviving domestic violence and finding love again with somebody new, it could be about a lot of things but rarely is it *just* about love.

If someone asks what your film's about, you might tell them the logline, a very short summary of the plot, but what is the meaning of that plot? What does it reveal about the human condition? What does it have to say?

The theme is your point of view about a specific aspect of a specific subject, whether it's love, money, greed, big business, racism, a political message, or whatever point you want to make about that specific topic. Think of theme as the moral message of the story.

Some people suggest that a screenplay (especially in some genres) doesn't really need to have a theme. They can even back up their claim with examples of successful films that are very entertaining but don't really have anything to say, and they would be correct. But, for the most part, human nature usually has us looking for the meaning of the story. And, since your audience will most likely try to find the meaning or message anyway, why not make sure that your story says exactly what you want it to say, rather than them guessing at what you really meant?

Your script may have an interesting premise and compelling characters, but if it's not "about" anything, if there isn't a deeper meaning, it may leave some audience members feeling a bit "cheated" because the story didn't completely satisfy their needs.

A script with a strong theme that has something to say will make your writing stand out, and it gives the actors something they can sink their teeth into. How often have you heard an actor say in an interview that *"The script really spoke to me"* or *"It had a message that needed to be told"* – that's the theme they are talking about. Not the dialogue, not the action sequences, not the locations or anything else… it's the theme.

When you know the theme of your story, write it on a sticky-note and put it on your monitor. If you get stuck on a scene, ask yourself if what you are writing supports the theme, or is it about something else? If it doesn't support the basic, underlying theme of your story, chances are it shouldn't be in your screenplay.

Writing some comic relief that doesn't support the theme is okay to use occasionally, but comic relief that somehow supports the theme is even better.

Theme Exercise # 1 – What's the Theme?

Pick 5 of your favorite movies. Using a sentence or a single word, write down what you believe is the theme of each movie.

Movie #1 Title: _____
Theme: _____

Movie #2 Title: _____
Theme: _____

Movie #3 Title: _____
Theme: _____

Movie #4 Title: _____
Theme: _____

Movie #5 Title: _____
Theme: _____

Theme Exercise # 2 – Think Outside the Box

Is there a common thread (theme or genre) in your list?

If your favorite movies have similar themes (or they're all the same genre) there's a good chance that your screenplay will have a similar theme and genre. I challenge you to think outside the box and <u>write a story around a theme or genre that you Do Not Like.</u>

For example, if you really dislike romances, then the challenge is to write a short romance story. It only has to be a few paragraphs long but don't just write silly fluff… take this exercise seriously and make it the best romance you can write.

No one but you will read it so don't worry about being embarrassed if it's not very good.

This writing exercise is designed to stretch your creative legs by forcing you to think and write outside your comfort zone.

Plus, if you decide to write a feature-length movie, the majority of the time there is some type of love interest as one of the subplots. You'll never have to struggle with how to write those romance scenes because you already tackled the subject and did some romance writing in this exercise.

Born in the trenches of low and no-budget filmmaking by an active indie filmmaker, **The Fundamentals of Screenwriting and Story Structure** won't waste your time with irrelevant and outdated theory – you learn what you really need to know to turn your ideas into short films.

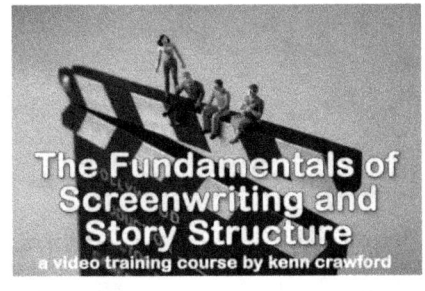

I know this stuff works because it's exactly how I write and shoot my short films on a budget of coffee and donuts!

What You'll Learn:
- How to write a screenplay that people want to read, and actors want to be in!
- How to create compelling characters that people will get emotionally invested in
- How to write believable dialogue
- How and Why to use suspense, drama and conflict
- You will learn the Screenwriting Elements you need to know, how to properly format and use them, and so much more!

The trainer talks everything through his experiences, that's the best part of it. I am going to come back and listen to everything again, the information he provides is vast. Loved the Bonus Podcasts at the end. ~ Jayachandran	Kenn is a REALLY GREAT instructor. I love how this course was just right. It had ALL the pertinent information, the encouragement without being too long. He is great to respond to questions. Thank you Kenn! I loved this course! ~ Rita	Really helped me pull together my thoughts on some script ideas. Seeing a few of Kenn's own films made it all come together for me. Thank you. ~ Susan

For more information visit:
kenncrawford.com/how-to-write-screenplay

Loglines

There is a difference between a logline and a tagline. A logline is a one (or two) sentence description that boils the entire script down to its essential dramatic narrative, while a tagline is a marketing tool, the hook, designed to go on the poster.

Many industry professionals recommend that you write the logline before you begin writing the screenplay itself. Why? Because if the logline is causing you problems, the script will cause you problems too.

For the movie ALIEN, the tagline is: *In space no one can hear you scream.*

For JAWS the tagline was: *You'll never go in the water again.*

The first tagline certainly evokes a sense of isolation, dread and menace. The second also suggests the same feelings of terror, and both grab your attention. Coming up with a catchy tagline for your story is important, especially when you're self-promoting your indie film on social media, but it is the logline that tells us what the movie is actually about.

The logline for THE MATRIX is: *A computer hacker learns from mysterious rebels about the true nature of his reality and his role in the war against its controllers.*

The logline for SILENCE OF THE LAMBS is: *A young F.B.I. cadet must confide in an incarcerated and manipulative killer to receive his help on catching another serial killer who skins his victims.*

Both of those loglines sum up the movies and makes you want to learn more. Movie execs are extremely busy and don't have the time to read every script that crosses their desk; they just want to know what the movie is about, and that's where the logline comes into play. It's your elevator pitch for your feature-length script.

If the exec likes the logline, they'll read the one-page synopsis. If they like that they'll read the script.

Needless to say, a great logline is critical to opening industry doors.

Learning how to write loglines now, even for short films, will help you hone your skills.

Plus, it'll help you promote your short film on social media.

These tips will help you write better loglines:

1. **A logline should have the following:**
   - ❖ the protagonist
   - ❖ their goal
   - ❖ the antagonist/antagonistic force

2. Don't use a character name.

Some movies do use character names, but for the most part there is no intrinsic value and is pretty much a useless word in a logline. So rather than just telling us the character's name, tell us something _about_ the character.

Examples:

A computer hacker	The aging patriarch
A young FBI cadet	An American expatriate
An incarcerated and manipulative killer	A wheelchair bound photographer

Some loglines do include character names, but as mentioned, the preferred method is to tell us about the character rather than their name.

Here are some examples with the character name in the logline:

> *Forrest Gump, while not intelligent, has accidentally been present at many historic moments, but his true love, Jenny, eludes him.* (FORREST GUMP)

> *Blacksmith Will Turner teams up with eccentric pirate "Captain" Jack Sparrow to save his love, the governor's daughter, from Jack's former pirate allies, who are now undead.* (PIRATES OF THE CARIBBEAN: THE CURSE OF THE BLACK PEARL)

> *During the U.S.-Vietnam War, Captain Willard is sent on a dangerous mission into Cambodia to assassinate a renegade colonel who has set himself up as a god among a local tribe.* (APOCALYPSE NOW)

3. Use an adjective to give a little depth to that character.

This is your chance to tell us something about the character.

A reclusive ex-boxer, an alcoholic ex-cop, a shy singer – all of these gives us a little insight into the character and into the story itself.

4. Quickly present the protagonist's main goal. Be clear and don't use questions.

The protagonist's goal is what drives your story, and it will drive your logline too.

> *A reclusive ex-boxer steps into the limelight one last time to save his daughter's life.*

5. Describe the Antagonist.

The antagonist should be described in a similar but shorter manner as the protagonist.

> *A reclusive ex-boxer is forced into the limelight by a sleazy promoter who kidnapped his estranged daughter.*

6. Make sure your protagonist is pro-active.

The protagonist should drive the story. In some cases, the protagonist will be reactive, but this is not the same as being passive.

7. If your story warrants it, include the stakes that are at risk.

Telling them what's at risk adds a sense of urgency to your script. If you can fit it in your logline you should include it.

8. Don't give away the ending.

Do not reveal the script's ending. Ever! I love writing surprise endings but including them in the logline is like telling the punchline before the joke.

9. Don't tell the story, sell the story.

The goal of the logline is to create a burning desire to read the script, not just to tell them what the story is about. Give your logline the time and respect it deserves. When you have a logline that tells the reader your screenplay is worth reading, you have a story worth writing.

Logline Exercise – Write Your Logline

If you already have a great idea for a screenplay, now is the time to write your logline.

If your idea for a movie is unfocused and confusing at the logline stage, it's not going to get any better when you write the script.

Not all ideas are destined to be great movies. Weed these out by first writing a great logline.

On the next page, fill out the information and use it to help you write a logline that makes people want to see your movie.

Title or the Basic Story Idea you have for a Film:

_____

The Protagonist:

_____

Their Goal:

_____

_____

The Antagonist or Antagonistic Force:

_____

The Logline:

_____

_____

_____

That's a Wrap!

I hope you enjoyed this book, but please allow me to leave you with this final piece of advice…

Knowledge is not power - it is only potential power. **The real power is action!** It is only when you take what you have learned and put it to use will you truly benefit from this book. I urge you to do the exercises, take what you have learned from these pages, then write and shoot something amazing.

Can I ask you for a small favor?

If you liked this book, please leave a review so other people may benefit from your experience. It really helps me as an indie author. You can use the link below to be taken directly to the page to rate and review this book.

Thank you,

Kenn

Use this link to leave a review:

kenncrawford.com/review10things

Thank you for your support

www.ingramcontent.com/pod-product-compliance
Lightning Source LLC
Chambersburg PA
CBHW071101240526
45471CB00016B/2301